Looking at Cathedrals BY NICHOLAS TAYLOR

CONTENTS

INTRODUCTION

The twenty-seven great cathedrals of England and Wales are now regarded by many Christians as millstones, pastorally, liturgically, and financially. As private bodies, unsupported by the state, they have their begging bowls fully extended: York for £2,000,000 (less than fifteen years after raising £250,000); Lincoln, £300,000; Norwich, £300,000; Bristol, £300,000; Exeter, £298,000; Chichester, £600,000; Winchester, £405,000. The enormity of such fund-raising seems out of all proportion to the liturgical value of those vast aisles on special occasions. Day-to-day services occupy only the choir stalls and the side chapels, while personal contact between priest and people, as at the confessional, is positively deterred by grandeur. Whatever romantic Liverpool may have done, it is significant that Coventry Cathedral and the proposed Roman Catholic Cathedral at Clifton are only of parish church size — and at a time when many people are questioning the suitability even of parish churches for the informal Christian supper.

Liturgically, the Deans and Chapters of the reformed Church of England have attempted to camp out in the shells of the great medieval Catholic cathedrals (and modern Catholics would find this no easier). The result aesthetically has been rape upon rape — what Mr Peter Anson slyly calls *Fashions in Church Furnishings*. At least Gilbert Scott's remodelling at Lichfield in the 1860s was full-blooded and became something valid in its own right. Since the last war, except at Chichester and Llandaff, the ancient cathedrals have been lulled by the anaesthetics of 'good taste': floral hassocks handwoven by the Friends, neo-Geo altar rails presented by the Freemasons, pale yellow stained glass of St Michael and the Bomber Pilots.

Yet the medieval cathedral has been one of the most passionate (and sometimes least tasteful) contributions this country has made to Western culture. For almost a thousand years, until the Reformation, the cathedrals were the chief promoters of English education, English painting, English libraries, English sculpture, English music – and music has since flourished under their wing for another four hundred years. Religion has now become just one of many specialized subjects. Beneath the Anglican mothballs we have to try to recapture in our imagination the total world for which these buildings were built. We have to imagine an intricate iconography of Heaven and Hell, picked out in flickering candlelight on buildings that, like the Parthenon, were painted in savagely bright colours; and we have to picture them dominating remote rural settlements at a time when wolves still roamed, disease was rife, and roads were muddy tracks. We have to try to imagine what the twenty-seven cathedral cities were like, as in the title of Le Corbusier's book, *When the Cathedrals Were White*.

Before losing ourselves in the guide book minutiae of antiquarian curiosity – scratch dials, lowside windows, hagioscopes, etc., etc. – we need to ask the same simple, and immensely complicated questions about each great church. Who built it? When? How did he pay for it? Where did the materials come from? What sort of man was the designer? Above all, why was it built as it was? What was the purpose of it all?

We need to ask these questions about great European monuments in not too insular a frame of mind. Bishop Gower's Palace at St Davids has a fantastic exterior with chequered stone, arcaded parapets, and rose windows; neither the detailed Ministry of Works guide book nor even Professor Webb's account in the Pelican History of Art, mention or explain its apparent similarity to Italian Gothic. How did Italy directly or indirectly come to Pembrokeshire? I don't know, but as a journalist I ask. More serious is the tendency among writers on cathedrals to discount the value of the work of William of Sens at Canterbury. Mr John Harvey, for example, says that 'the new French Canterbury was a retrograde step; the periapsidal plan and Corinthianesque columns of France were imported as they stood'. Yet this was surely not a bad idea, considering that France had invented the Gothic style of architecture thirty-five years earlier and that its advantages had not been fully imported into this country; in any case, William of Sens adapted his French ideas very considerably to salvage existing buildings and to give long and low proportions.

We have always been an offshore island – in good times able to borrow without strings (as at Canterbury or Westminster Abbey) and at bad times shut off (as during the fifteenth and sixteenth century Renaissance). It is the cosmopolitan mingling of traditions, in an island which has always depended for its prosperity on overseas trade and on immigration, that has given the English cathedrals their distinctive pattern. Of overseas influences, the earliest were no doubt the most lasting and at the same time the least evident in actual buildings today; and it is these which are worth introducing here.

St Augustine in 597 came as a missionary direct from Rome, bringing with him the Benedictine order of monasticism, with its emphasis on communal buildings planned as a unity, and the Roman idea of the church building as a symmetrical shrine, set back like a Pompeian house, within a walled or cloistered atrium for visitors. Whereas most Greek and early Roman temples were external structures with only a small inner sanctum for the priest, Christians stressed the participation of all their members in congregational worship. They therefore adopted the kind of long rooms which had been used as temples by the newer 'mystery' religions from the East such as Mithraism and as basilicas or assembly halls by the Roman cities. Most of the churches built after Constantine made Christianity the official religion of the Empire in 313 were basilican, with round-headed arcades marching relentlessly onward to the east end, where the judge's seat was replaced appropriately by the altar table. An apse was added with the bishop's throne in its centre, facing the people over the altar – a position which only Norwich now preserves in this country; it was flanked by the seats of the priests, an arrangement deriving from the Jewish synagogue. The grandest English basilica to survive from the years immediately after St Augustine is the parish church of Brixworth near Northampton.

In the North by contrast the Irish missionaries had landed, founding the monasteries of Northumbria. As can still be seen at Glendalough or Monasterboice in Ireland, they consisted of wholly irregular clusters of small stone huts for the individual monks interspersed with small square-ended chapels. This was an idea St Patrick derived from Egypt, where groups of hermits called coenobites had gathered together. At certain focal points, the Irish built tall belfries, where treasures could be stored when under attack, and richly sculptured High Crosses, which were a kind of Christian takeover of the megalith. From these apparently ramshackle – and in a Roman sense unarchitectural – places came the great illuminated books of Lindisfarne and Jarrow.

When English missionaries such as Boniface and Willibrord converted Upper Germany, they helped to prepare the way for a third major influence on their own homeland: Charlemagne's establishment of the Holy Roman Empire in 800. Charlemagne built a number of major churches and reassessed the various types of post-Constantinian church. His palace chapel at Aachen derived its centralized polygonal plan from San Vitale in Ravenna and it in turn influenced the rotunda at St Augustine's Canterbury (see page 4). His church at Fulda derived from the T-shaped basilicas at Rome (St Peter's and St Paul's) which had a deep transept between nave and apse; this plan appears in England at the little-known ruins of the cathedral at North Elmham, Norfolk (Elmham was Norwich's predecessor as the seat of East Anglia's bishopric). The Old Minster recently excavated at Winchester (971–94) also shows Carolingian influence, in its exceptionally deep apse, with two apsidal chapels on each side. It also had a western transept similar to the *westwerk* of German cathedrals – a feature first introduced in the abbey of Centula built for Charlemagne's son-in-law (790–9).

North Elmham is now our only surviving Saxon cathedral, small and ruined. So ruthlessly did the Normans introduce their government of grandeur, that we know very little about other, and more important, early cathedrals; yet one suspects that they must have shown in embryo some of the traits of character which, barely a hundred years after their demolition, appeared in Early English Gothic in sharp contradistinction to the Continent. One thing is certain: the Saxons sited most of their cathedrals in villages; as can still be seen at Wells (see page 22) and St Davids. Even within the Roman grid pattern at those towns the Saxons had inherited, such as York and Winchester, the Cathedral Close from an early date was a haven of informality. The Normans decided in council at Windsor (1072) that cathedrals should henceforth be in walled towns, not in villages. Yet even within walls, the detachment from the city of the English cathedral community is a remarkable phenomenon, totally different from the involvement of the cathedral in the market place which is familiar on the Continent. Ruskin described this difference brilliantly in *The Stones of Venice* when he compared a typically somnolent English Close with the clattering and raucous approach to St Mark's. During the eighteenth century there had descended on the Closes a deep sleep, fortified by rich medieval endowments (Trollope describes the atmosphere); the latter were finally confiscated by the Ecclesiastical Commissioners in 1884, so that standard salaries could be paid and the remaining profits used for the Church as a whole.

The Dean and Chapter as an independent corporation was an innovation by the Normans (*c.* 1086); previously the Bishop had been directly in charge, but his increasing duties in State as well as Church made it necessary for him to delegate authority. However, with the growth of pilgrimages and the increasing veneration of saints, the Chapters became exceedingly powerful bodies and were often in conflict with the Bishop whom they had actually, or nominally, elected. The cathedrals of the Old Foundation such as York and Salisbury were staffed by 'secular' canons — that is to say, ordinary non-monastic priests. There were three principal officials under the Dean: the Precentor organized the services of worship; the Chancellor ran the cathedral school and other educational work; the Treasurer acted as curator of valuables. Some powerful cathedrals, however, were centred on a great Benedictine monastery, as at Durham and Canterbury; here the Prior was in charge until the Reformation, when Henry VIII re-established these cathedrals with Deans and Chapters — known as the New Foundation.

Significantly, Chapter Houses and choir stalls are invariably among the best organized designs; the Chapter Houses in particular give a spatial expression of meeting in common which is much more decisive than that in the actual places of worship. The Chapters presided over the continuous evolution in the design of cathedrals which is illustrated in the following pages. There was *structural* evolution, from the massive walls and round arches of the Romanesque to the slim shafts and pointed vaults of Late Gothic. There was *sculptural* evolution, from the rude grandeur of Lincoln's west front with its scenes of snakes biting off men's vitals, to the sweetness and humanity of the Angel Choir, a hundred and forty years and four hundred feet away. There was *liturgical* evolution — vitally important — in the need for small altars (the Abbey of Cluny in Burgundy had begun the practice of daily Mass for each priest), in the growing emphasis on processions to a great saint's shrine behind the High Altar, and in the contrasting need for friars to be able to preach in big open rooms to the minds and emotions of ordinary men. There was *philosophical* evolution, from the early emphasis by writers such as Anselm on general Platonic principles of order to the later scholastic advocacy of Aristotle's theory that only individual manifestations were real. There was *scientific* evolution towards mathematical and geometrical systems of harmony and proportion.

All this was evolution, not revolution, for the medieval belief in God's revelation meant that eternal truth was uncovered, bit by bit, rather than new truths discovered, suddenly. Paul Frankl calls this an 'immanent process'. No specialized department of engineering or philosophy by itself invented the diagonal spaces of a Gothic cathedral. The architect's job is always synthetic, putting things together into a physical unity; the medieval master masons superintended construction as well as design. Only gradually do we begin to learn their names because of their low social status as craftsmen. A masons' lodge at a cathedral would influence the surrounding region; and the master mason would increasingly travel to superintend other jobs. The client, in the form of the Bishop or the Dean and Chapter, probably played more part in design than he would today; but the Gothic vault was nevertheless a technicians' job — only indirectly the result of philosophy or liturgy or prayer. The medieval cathedrals were works of piety only in the general sense that they were intended as the symbols of religious power (theocracy). The power of God and the power of aristocratic status were reconciled, not always consistently, in the prince-bishop; meanwhile the friars began the process of questioning which led ultimately to the Reformation and the attempt to detach religion from semi-secular pomp. In the High Gothic period of the thirteenth century, however, there was a precarious unity of Church and State, religion and feudalism, pastoral care and aristocracy. In the cathedrals we can see a gradual evolution of the individual personality of the artist, and the attempt to establish a hierarchical relationship between him and society ('partiality', as Frankl puts it, as against the all-submerging 'totality' of the Romanesque).

The special contribution of the English cathedrals lies in fact in their stress on the individual part — on the 'additive' principle of building up a great building, such as Salisbury, hierarchically out of small boxes. This sometimes led to lamentable confusion (the three different styles in the nave of St Albans, for example) compared with the effortless control and single-mindedness of the great French cathedrals. The English tried to control the centrifugal tendencies of individualism by stressing great length — uniformly horizontal roofs, instead of the aspiring verticals of France — and, by contrast, great towers (the Irish influence of long before). There is also an English habit of disciplining surfaces by standardized grids, as in the Perpendicular style. Remoulding informally the architectural inventions of the Continent — first the Romanesque and then the Gothic — the English masons evolved buildings with a human appeal which has outlived their narrowly defined usefulness.

Ethelbert, King of Kent, was baptized by St Augustine in 597; the eleventh-century font at St Martin's church, Canterbury, is on the site where the ceremony took place.

The footworn treads of the Pilgrim Steps, **1**, rise to the climactic curve of arches round the site of St Thomas Becket's shrine. Pilgrimages were popular carnivals with a serious end; their badges, banners, slogans, community singing and impromptu oratory are familiar to us from the Aldermaston marches. Canterbury's master masons showed an unequalled gift for translating them into an architecture of movement: an almost endless sequence of aisles, passages, crypts and cloisters.

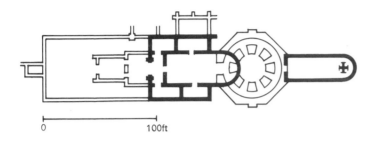

St Augustine's Abbey, Saxon plan, with earlier work in black

Nothing survives of St Augustine's cathedral of 597, but, except that we deduce its nave had columns and arcades, it must have been similar to St Augustine's Abbey nearby, where we can still see fascinating foundations. A towered gateway led to a broad Roman atrium or forecourt, into which projected two successive porches (added later); beyond them lay the main abbey church, only 67 feet by 26 feet, which was in turn flanked by little *porticus* (or porch-chapels) containing the bones of the first archbishop-saints and the Kentish royal family. A few yards to the east was a second church; the space between was filled by Abbot Wulfric (*c.* 1055–9) with a remarkable rotunda, of the type derived from Charlemagne's Palace Chapel at Aachen and Justinian's San Vitale at Ravenna; the immediate influence was St Bénigne, Dijon.

The Cathedral Church of Christ was also a monastery, ruled by a prior. Archbishop Lanfranc built a massive aisled basilica (*c.* 1070–7) on the typical cruciform plan. The choir was doubled in size as early as 1096–1107, with eastern transepts on the pattern of Cluny (where rebuilding was completed in 1095); of this 'Glorious Choir of Conrad', designed by the master mason, Blitherus, the largest Romanesque crypt in Europe survives almost intact, **5**. It has a multitude of altars glimpsed through a forest of columns; their capitals are carved with beasts and abstract foliage in the style of ivories or manuscripts. Above it, only parts of the eastern transepts and the two eastern chapels of St Andrew and St Anselm survived the great fire of 1174.

Four years earlier (1170) Thomas Becket had been murdered; he was a worldly courtier of Henry II who had turned unexpectedly into an extremist champion of the Church's independent power. Men of religion who only eight years earlier had resisted his nepotistic appointment as Archbishop did not scruple to exploit his martyrdom for the sake of humiliating the rising power of the State. The gold-plated shrine, designed in 1220 by two artistic priests, Walter de Colecestria and Elias de Derham, put the final touch to a centre of pilgrimage which was advertised throughout Europe, and was, not surprisingly, destroyed by Henry VIII. The superb sanctuary which enclosed it, **3**, is the work of a Frenchman, William of Sens, who here introduced to England the Gothic style, invented at St Denis, and used already in the cathedral at William's home town. French are the Corinthian columns, **4**, almost Roman in their gravity; French are the sexpartite vaults (fireproof) with their emphatic division into structural bays supported by flying buttresses; French is the idea of an apsidal Gothic choir. William, however, was responsive to local demands: to the English desire for processional length rather than aspiring height; to the use of the new English luxury material of Purbeck marble in a multiplicity of little black shafts; above all, to the monks' desire (typical of English conservatism) that he should salvage all he could of Conrad's choir. The two chapels of St Andrew and St Anselm, canted inwards round Conrad's apse, are allowed to squeeze the new choir inwards to the High Altar (next to the Pilgrim Steps); then the whole building swells outwards again for the Trinity Chapel at a higher level, which enclosed the shrine of St Thomas. In 1180 William died after a fall from the scaffolding; his successor, William the Englishman, faithfully completed the work with the astonishing horseshoe-shaped Corona, **2**, enclosing the ceremonial Chair of St Augustine. Round ambulatory and Corona are superb stained glass windows in the style of Chartres, with subjects from the Bible and from the miracles of St Thomas.

Lanfranc's nave was rebuilt in 1379–1405 by the King's Master Mason, Henry Yevele; it is a supreme example of the English Perpendicular style, **7**, in which the strength of the vaulting shafts and the height of the aisles almost create a 'hall church' (Bristol, page 26). Yevele and his successor Stephen Lote rebuilt the main cloisters, displaying in the elaborate lierne vault the heraldry of Kentish families who subscribed. Lote completed the proud Chapter House with a star-patterned roof of wood second only to Westminster Hall in size. From a passage alongside is reached an extensive eastern sequence of twelfth century vaulted cloisters, **8**, culminating in the remarkable polygonal water tower of Prior Wibert (1160). The buildings of King's School contain many other monastic remains including the much restored Norman Strangers' Hall, where poor pilgrims slept at the top of an incredibly luxurious stair, **9**, reflecting the almost Oriental prosperity of religious tourism. The final touch, perfectly proportioned, is the central tower, **6**, known as Bell Harry; it was designed in 1490–7 by John Wastell, the master mason who also created the fan vaulting of King's College, Cambridge.

Note: the figures on the plans mark the viewpoints of the photographic illustrations, with arrows indicating the direction of the more distant places.

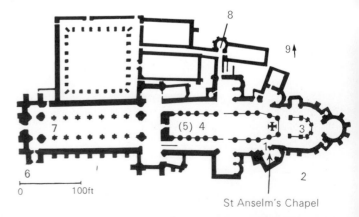

St Anselm's Chapel

The climax to the Canterbury pilgrimage is now a void, **3**, enclosed by the apse of the Trinity Chapel, which carries consistently eastward the whole height of the choir. Only the rich pavement survives – said to be spoil from the notorious Fourth Crusade. Between the arches of the ambulatory can be seen the so-called Corona, or Becket's Crown, which shelters the ceremonial Chair of St Augustine. The strangely undulating walls are explained externally, **2**, by the way in which William of

2

3

Sens preserved the side chapels of St Andrew and St Anselm (left of picture), which had been canted inwards round the apse of the previous choir of Conrad. So the cathedral is first pinched inwards and then expands outwards again to enclose St Thomas's shrine – a solution as emphatic as it is economic. The final twist is the Corona of William the Englishman. The scale of its two flanking stair turrets suggests that they originally supported steeples, but these were swept away when the monks made an attempt in the 1530s to carry up the whole structure as an eastern tower,

4

5

6

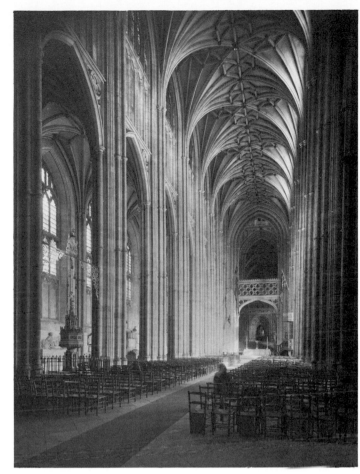

7

hence the eccentric silhouette. The flood of pilgrims was so great that it disturbed the monks' singing of the Offices, so Prior Eastry had the traceried parclose screens, **4**, built in 1300. The single shafts of the main arcade show a characteristically French emphasis on logical structure. Beneath the choir, **5**, is the largest Romanesque crypt in Europe, built mainly by Prior Ernulf, Conrad's predecessor. The endless groined vaulting contrasts with the fantastic capitals. No less extensive are the Norman cloisters which lie between the main cloister and King's School, converging on the complicated substructure, **8**, of the Water Tower built by Prior Wibert (1160). The poor pilgrims slept in Strangers' Hall (now King's School library), **9**, reached through this elaborate Norman stairway. The nave, **6**, was rebuilt from 1379 by Henry Yevele and the central tower, Bell Harry, in 1490–7 by John Wastell. The eastern transept and staircase tower of Conrad's choir survive to the right. The interior of Yevele's nave, **7**, is the climax of the English Perpendicular style, its unemotional lightness and verticality forming a complete contrast to the awesome east end.

8

9

DURHAM

Held by the jaws of a ferocious beast, whose eyes originally flashed in enamel, the twelfth-century door knocker of Durham, **1**, with its power of giving sanctuary to the fugitive, sums up the hold over life and death of a prince-bishop who (as in Germany) ruled an almost independent County Palatine. *Quicquid rex habet extra, episcopus habet intra* (the king's prerogatives without are the bishop's within). As a border fortress, Durham's castle, cathedral and monastery crown the cliffs on a horseshoe bend of the Wear, **2**, with the triumphant skyline of a German *stadtkröne* — a thrilling sight in England, where by protection the sea has allowed most towns peacefully to sprawl. Furthermore the cathedral is massively unified in design: except for the Early English Chapel of the Nine Altars which forms a distinctive T-shaped eastern end and the tapering Perpendicular central tower, almost everything we see was built in forty years, between 1093 and 1133. As Pevsner says, 'What gives [Durham] supremacy over all other Norman buildings in England or Normandy is this unexpected combination of primeval power, the power of William's conquest and of his bloody conquest of the north, with a consummate mastery of scale and proportion'.

It is on the face of it an unlikely place to find the relics of St Cuthbert (died 687) and of the Venerable Bede (died 735). In the former monastic dormitory are displayed St Cuthbert's pectoral cross of gold cloisonné and his coffin of oak incised with figures of Christ, the Virgin and the angels; the linear draughtsmanship, a synthesis of Irish and Roman, has a soft and mystical melancholy appropriate to a hermit-bishop. These relics, together with some superb eighth-century manuscripts, were concealed by devoted monks during the Viking raids.

Ultimate security against fire as well as war was given to the relics with Europe's first rib vault in stone. The Roman art of vaulting, carried almost to perfection by Justinian at Santa Sophia, was utterly lost in the barbarian invasions. Besides reflecting the cave or catacomb tradition in Christian worship, it gave aesthetic unity to a great church in its role as a symbol of Heaven on Earth. The tunnel vaults of Tournus in Burgundy (*c.* 1010) and the groin vaults of Speier on the Rhine (*c.* 1085) pressed evenly as a dead weight so that columns and walls had to be immensely thick. Durham made the crucial innovation of the rib vault which in less than fifty years led to the engineering of light-weight Gothic at St Denis near Paris.

In the first great Norman churches the arches were merely repetitive holes in solid wall, as at St Albans; then they became differentiated equally repetitively by a series of tall stone 'masts' rising direct from floor to wooden ceiling, as at Ely or Peterborough. At Durham the arches are fully expressed individually as such, in a series of double bays. Alternate columns are circular, with patterns of spirals and zigzags, and clustered, in groups of shafts, round a cruciform core. The clustered columns carry on one side the familiar mast; but when it meets the ceiling it carries on and over as an enormous arch, 73 feet high and 39 feet wide, spanning the nave transversely to join up with the parallel mast on the other side. The familiar three-storey elevations of arcade, gallery (mis-called triforium) and clerestory are here turned into more than elevations — into a single interconnecting space — by these transverse arches. Between each pair of them are two bays of groin vaulting, each divided up by strong ribs into four cells (quadripartite).

Rib vaults were found to be easier to build. The immense

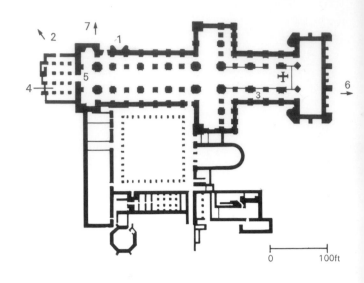

structure of wooden scaffolding known as 'centering', which in a tunnel vault had to be built up to support the construction of every inch of masonry, was here needed only for the ribs, with lighter scaffolding for the masons who inserted the cells of infilling. In any variety of Romanesque, however, such as the Anglo-Norman, the use of semi-circular arches throughout led to obvious problems. In the single-storey aisles, the longitudinal and transverse arches were of a similar height, and the bays were square in plan; although the diagonal ribs had to be longer and flatter, the distortion was not so acute as to endanger the structure. In a three-storey nave, however, when the transverse arches had to be wider, the bays became oblong; the diagonal ribs, therefore, had to be still longer, and their arches were stretched and flattened out. This is a dangerous shape structurally — too much dead weight pressing on a flat arch — and it is not surprising that the main choir vault, the first to be built, had to be renewed in 1280. It is in the choir aisles that the earliest rib vaults now survive, **3**; those in the transepts also miraculously survive, though confusing details in the elevations show that after the death of Bishop William of St Carileph in 1096 the monks for a time had second thoughts about their first master mason's bravado.

So in the somewhat belated nave vault, **5**, constructed in 1128–33, two crucial changes were made, one easily seen, the other unseen. In order to allow the diagonal ribs to become semi-circular, the transverse arches had to be either stilted or pointed, and the Durham masons structurally and visually preferred to make them pointed. (Cluny and Autun in France had come to the same conclusion in the years since the choir vault had been built.) Secondly, in the gallery, invisible to the public, the subsidiary transverse arches which in the chancel were conventionally semicircular are here turned into half arches — in effect, into flying buttresses (which French cathedrals had used only to abut tunnel vaults). At St Denis in 1140–4, all these elements came together in the new Gothic style, and this was imported into England at Canterbury in 1175.

2

As the capital of an almost independent County Palatine, Durham's cathedral and castle, **2**, are an aggressive display of strength on the Scottish border. The River Wear encircles the horseshoe-shaped promontory with steep cliffs. The quadripartite vaults of the choir aisles, **3**, begun in 1093, are the earliest ribbed vaults in Europe. The nave vault, **5**, of 1128–33, is a prelude to the development of Gothic architecture: the high transverse arches are made pointed so as not to flatten the diagonal ribs dangerously. The

3

4

immense and ornate piers (the nearest on the left has the typical Norman cushion capitals) are matched in scale by the remarkable 40 foot font cover presented by Bishop Cosin in 1663. The skinny rose window to the east is by James Wyatt, 1795; it lights the gorgeous eastern transept (1247–80), known as the Chapel of the Nine Altars. The rugged response of Durham to its rocky setting has recently been enhanced, **6**, by the beautiful foot-bridge designed for the University by Ove Arup, and by Dunelm House (the University Clubhouse), a massively monolithic structure of rough-shuttered concrete, designed by Architects' Co-Partnership. The most powerful Norman bishop was Hugh de Puiset,

5   6

nephew of Queen Matilda, and his architecture shows the degree of savage luxury a warrior-bishop could enjoy. He built out the Galilee Chapel, 4, on the cliff top to the west of the nave. Its quatrefoil columns are of almost Roman simplicity and the high blank walls above subdivide the interior with classical neatness (there is no sense yet of the diagonal pull of Gothic vaulting); but every surface must originally have been richly painted. Within the Castle, now University College, de Puiset built a new chapel and hall; above the hall is the Constable's Hall, 7, known as the Norman Gallery; its lavish window seats have a remarkably plastic alternation of wall, window, and column.

7

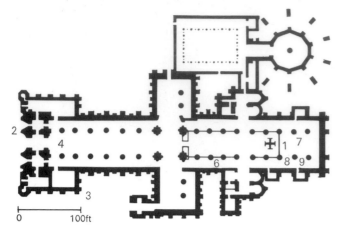

The Angel Choir of Lincoln, 1, completed in 1280, is the climax of an 'age of equipoise' — one of those rare moments in history (1470 in Florence, 1870 in Birmingham) when the leaders of articulate opinion precariously achieved a 'world view', reconciling art and science, civilization and nature, man and God. Lincoln's Norman cathedral collapsed in 1185 and only its west front now survives, 2. A year later Henry II boldly commanded the Chapter to elect as bishop an unworldly monk, St Hugh of Avalon; he had been treasurer of the Grande Chartreuse. The new austere monastic orders disliked the luxuriant curves of the French *chevet* of apses; the Cistercians under St Bernard brought back into England the flat east end which the Saxons had preferred, and the Carthusians (St Hugh's order) broke down the grandiose unity of the Benedictine monastery into a series of straight-sided cells. More important, St Bernard's preaching about individual morality re-awakened that personal originality of the Saxon artists which the Norman administrative steamroller had flattened. The new Gothic style, which concentrated its weight on points of tension with great areas of diaphanous glazing between, became the architectural expression of the heavenly spheres, about which the university schoolmen at Paris and Oxford were speculating.

St Hugh's *constructor a fundamentis*, Geoffrey de Noiers (of French name but English sympathies) began in 1192 a design which, as it evolved over eighty-eight years, became the classic synthesis of Saxon and Gothic. The most French feature of Geoffrey's was an eastern *chevet* of apsed chapels, but these were attached to a tapered rectangle rather than a polygon — and they were all removed when the fame of St Hugh's own shrine paid for the Angel Choir. It is in the eastern transepts — that characteristic toasting fork of altars (derived from Cluny) which satisfied the Saxon tradition of emphatic orientation — that Geoffrey's originality can best be appreciated. He took the French idea of the detached

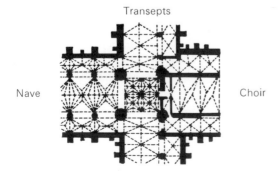

Transepts

Nave   Choir

The vaults of Lincoln

marble shaft (used by William of Sens at Canterbury) and transformed it from structural logic into flickering mysticism. In Geoffrey's extraordinary wall-arcading, 6, an inner layer of conventionally pointed limestone arches is overlaid by an alternating outer layer of gracefully trefoiled arches on Purbeck shafts, producing a skipping syncopated rhythm. Geoffrey was not worried by exact measurements: his wall arcading slap-happily bangs into bay divisions and there are curious cramped arches in the corners. There is great variety in the clustering of columns and vaulting ribs in the side chapels. But the most astonishing feature is the roof of the choir, which Paul Frankl called the Crazy Vault of Lincoln, and which Pevsner says was 'the first ribbed vault with purely decorative intentions'. Decisive division between vaulting bays, the key to the logical unity of a French cathedral, 5, is here given up in favour of a palm frond effect of ribs outspringing from that very point of division — syncopation again. In Lincoln choir this is gleefully exaggerated by adding an extra rib called a tierceron to one side only of each palm frond, splitting up the other ribs irregularly and alternating this asymmetry from side to side (see plan).

The later masters at Lincoln slightly modified these oddities of Geoffrey in favour of something more solid — understandably, as they had to rebuild his tower when it collapsed after only thirty years. In the nave, 4, syncopation was adapted to an equally mystical continuity: an emphatic ridge rib ties the palm fronds together down the length of the church; the wall arcades in the aisles continue uninterrupted behind the wall shafts of the vaulting, and the blank lancets between the clerestory windows are equally undisturbed by the flying buttresses which punch into them, 3. The Angel Choir of 1256–80 made the whole church of equal width and height from flat end to flat end.

Such optical effects are characteristic of Early English speculation in philosophy as well as in art. Robert Grosseteste, the scientist-scholar of European reputation who was Bishop of Lincoln in 1235–53, had written in his treatise on optics that 'light is the most noble of natural phenomena, the least material, the closest approximation to pure form' and had described it as 'actually the mediator between bodiless and bodily substances, a spiritual body, an embodied spirit'. Lincoln has lost a great deal of this mediation between the human and the divine — that is, architecture expressed as a Sacrament — through the destruction by Puritans of almost all the stained glass except the fragments now gathered into the two famous rose windows of the transepts, Bishop's Eye and Dean's Eye. Without the mysterious atmosphere of medieval glass Lincoln's central spaces are, in spite of Geoffrey's brilliant detail, rather dull as a whole — thick and squat compared with a French cathedral, 4 and 5, and tending to fall into a series of attractive but separate parts. The spatial unity of the Angel Choir is partly recaptured by the neo-thirteenth-century glass of 1855 in the glorious Geometrical east window. Within this unity the Angel Choir's rich sculpture, 7–9 expresses the new freedom of the human spirit in which the thirteenth century preceded the Renaissance. The classical culture of internationally minded scholars from England, such as Duns Scotus, William of Occam and Robert Grosseteste is perfectly expressed in the twenty-eight angels between the gallery spandrels which give this choir its name: some are elegantly feminine in the style of Rheims and Westminster, others thickly masculine in a more realistic manner than the ideal bodies of the Renaissance.

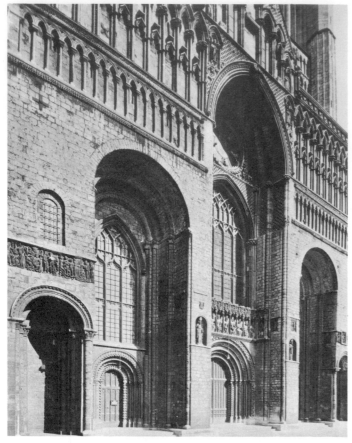

2

3

4

5

An Early English false screen frames a strange and brilliant Early Norman west front, surviving from Bishop Remigius's cathedral of 1075–92. Five niches, two small, two big, and one giant, express convincingly the relationship of nave, aisles, and chapels behind. The three doorways date from *c*. 1145, as do the friezes above them, which are in a North Italian style, similar to Modena Cathedral. The towers behind the screen wall are Remigius's in their lower stages. 3, with shallow projecting gables, highly ornamented. Unrestricted by the width of Remigius's front, the nave of *c*. 1225–33, 4, maintains the basic proportions of Lincoln set in St Hugh's choir: broad bays and spacious aisles without much height. Early English is conventionally regarded as a 'pure' style, but Lincoln abounds in surprises. The vault avoids not only the exhausting proportions of a French cathedral such as Amiens, 5, but also its logical division into structural bays. The heavy longitudinal ridge rib stresses continuity eastwards, and the palm fronds of tierceron ribs from each shaft move the emphatic break in the vault to the centre of each bay, so that there is an alternating relationship with the ground. The syncopated wall arcading to the choir aisle, 6, is a virtuoso display of stone masonry technique and fashionable Purbeck marble columns, while convincingly stressing the processional sense of movement inherent in a wall arcade. The Angel Choir (1256–80) is the climax of

6

the church, with extremely luxuriant carving. There are cascades of foliage between the spandrels of the main arcade, **7** (this one has the renowned Lincoln Imp sitting at its foot). The bosses of the vault show astonishing progress in human observation, over a century before the Renaissance. The pair of wrestlers, **8**, probably symbolizing good and evil, are modelled with a close regard for anatomy, and are gathered up by a frame of foliage into a *tondo* shape; while an aristocratic lady cuddles a puppy, **9**, without false sentiment.

7

8/9

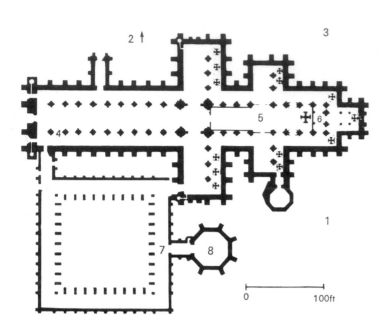

tic belief in harmony of proportion as an expression of God's creation. But this is not the static perfection of Renaissance symmetry. In High Gothic harmony is a balance of tensions, passionate belief held in a moment's perfect suspense. St Thomas Aquinas (in his *Summa*) said that beauty 'consists of a certain consonance of diverging elements'.

Elias's plan at Salisbury is essentially additive: a series of almost repetitive boxes, piled up as though prefabricated. The lack of vast single spaces in English cathedrals (as there are at Amiens, begun in the same year as Salisbury) is not the result of conservatism or shortage of money; for at Salisbury all except the spire, the cloister and the demolished campanile was built in 1220–58 as a single building operation. Work would have started at the east end where three altars were consecrated in 1225, presumably those of the Lady Chapel and chancel aisles. It is here, **6**, that Salisbury's perfection becomes for a moment breathtaking architecture in three dimensions and not just a diagram. Already the twelfth-century cathedral at Old Sarum had had a lower east end with apses enclosed in square ends, **2**; at nearby Winchester earlier than 1204, a Lady Chapel and retrochoir had been built as a single storey 'hall church' with aisles and nave vaulted at an equal height. The idea was later to be adopted at Bristol (see page 26) for a whole church. The Lady Chapel aisles at Salisbury have single 'stove pipe' shafts of Purbeck marble; the retrochoir has clusters of five and six, delicately detached from one another.

Externally too, **3**, the east end works superbly as a composition in projecting and receding masses with two tiers of lancet windows under each gable, the upper tier lighting a roof space over the vault. Groups of three lancets in the gable ends, groups of two in the sides, single ones for the Lady Chapel aisles and as niches for statues – and as many as seven in the chancel gable – these are composed in felicitously stepped formations, with occasional spandrels of plate tracery, in the walls of greyish green Chilmark stone.

It is the rest of the building which is increasingly uncomfortable, culminating in the clumsily ill-related screen of statues at the west front. One can only suppose that the executant master-mason did not share Elias's intellectual frame of mind and failed to grasp the importance of maintaining his rigour further west. The painful asymmetry of the one-aisled main transept is exacerbated by the insertion of broken half-arches at the sides of the stepped lancets. Internally, **4** and **5**, the main arcades of two kinds of Purbeck marble, black polished and grey unpolished, are beautifully handled, as is the soaring clerestory; but it is hard to credit the proportions of the squat and over-detailed gallery between. The French cathedrals had by this time resolved the problem by reducing the gallery to a narrow band of wall passage (the true triforium). Particularly uneasy are the east and west walls: the east wall with its three awkwardly unequal arches and its stumpy gallery, and the west wall with its total failure to relate its levels to those of the adjoining elevations. The difficulty of a 'pure' style is that it demands purity to the uttermost detail.

Cloisters, **7**, and chapter house, begun in c. 1270, are far more generously spatial in feeling, as is the exquisite tomb of Bishop Giles de Bridport (died 1262) which introduces to Salisbury the bar tracery of Westminster Abbey (and Reims before it). The octagonal chapter house, **8**, also deriving from Westminster, has a continuous band of carving from Genesis over the seats and splendid Geometrical windows overhead.

Like most new towns, **1**, Salisbury is more striking as a state of mind than as a work of architecture – apart from the glorious spire added over a hundred years later. 'Let us descend joyfully to the plains, where the valley abounds in corn, where the fields are beautiful and where there is freedom from oppression'. So exulted the Papal Bull of Honorius II in 1219, which authorized removal of the cathedral from the clutches of the hostile royal garrison of Old Sarum, **2**, where cathedral, castle and hill city jostled on the windswept, waterless summit. The city followed the bishop, and the castle finally fell into ruin.

Like that even older Wiltshire temple, Stonehenge, Salisbury is fascinating as an intellectual theorem. Although a master-mason called Nicholas of Ely was employed, there can be little doubt who the master mind was: Elias de Derham, canon of Salisbury. Present as a courtier at the signing of Magna Carta (of which Salisbury has one of the three surviving copies), he was one of the two *artifices incomparabiles* who designed the shrine of St Thomas at Canterbury; in the 1230s he was in charge of the rebuilding of the King's palaces at Clarendon and Winchester and, as a personal friend of Bishop Hugh II of Lincoln and Bishop Jocelyn of Wells, was evidently a central figure in the evolution of the so-called Court Style of Henry III which culminated in Westminster Abbey.

The essence of Salisbury is the grid: the city's streets are all at right angles, enclosing blocks called 'chequers', and, however overlaid this pattern has become with informally accretive buildings, it is still stunningly clear in the parallel plots of land for the canons' houses (background **1**), beyond which are the water meadows from which Constable painted. In the cathedral itself the parallelism must have appeared fanatical before the spire took it out of itself. The whole city is an expression of the thirteenth century scholas-

1

2

3

4

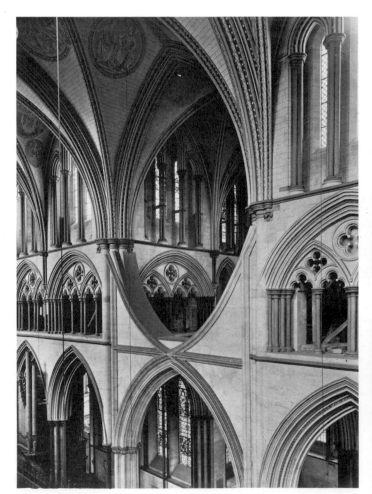

5

From the north east approach, **3**, the cathedral sits on a plain of mown grass which would completely lack reality were it not for the irregular weathering to a greyish green of the local Chilmark stone and for the distinctive personality of the tower and spire. From this viewpoint the additive formation of Early English Gothic is most apparent. The interior, **4**, is decidedly cool, but this is partly because of a lack of stained glass and mural painting to offset the black and grey uniform of Purbeck marble and Chilmark stone, and partly because of James Wyatt's rationalistic tidying of all the monuments into two parallel rows between the arcades. The height of 81 feet allows sufficient room for soaring arcades and equally soaring clerestory; but the triforium suffers middle-age spread in between, while being too large to be dismissed as a mere wall passage. Like the spire, the strainer arches, **5**, inserted into the eastern transepts for reasons of safety, are a relief from intellectual coolness. Much the most successful part of the original design is the retrochoir and Lady Chapel, **6**, where the designer seems to have had a vision of the later medieval hall church, with its cells of equal height and exquisitely slim columns of Purbeck marble. For a non-monastic cathedral, cloisters were a luxury; those at Salisbury, **7**, were added in c. 1270. The glass in the Chapter House windows, **8**, was recreated in 1856 by the Victorian architects, Clutton and Burges, who had discovered a fragment of the original; an attempt to remove it all in 1900 was scotched.

6

7   8

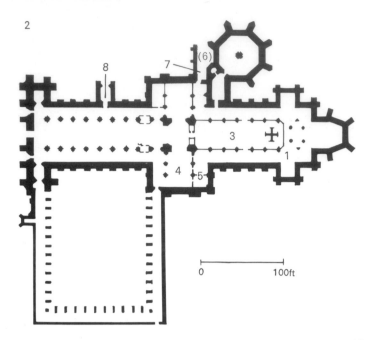

The poetry of Gothic architecture lies often in metaphors of its natural setting: at Venice of frozen sea-spray (Ruskin's idea), at Durham of rugged cliffs, at Wells's retrochoir of cultivated orchards, **1**. From the 'classical' composure of Lincoln's three-storey Angel Choir (page 13), the West Country master-masons pushed on for fifty years in developing diagonal space at one level only, through which the pilgrim could move in mystical freedom as through an enchanted forest. Between the fully developed structure of French High Gothic (Amiens, Beauvais), and the equally extreme flow of space in Central European Late Gothic (Nuremberg, Prague), the West of England is the bridge — one of only two times in history when we have led Europe in the mainstream of architectural ideas (the other was in the 1890s, when we produced middle-class houses with a similar sensitivity to natural forms).

Approached from Glastonbury through the thick-carpeted greenery of the Vale of Avalon, Wells sits back against the Mendips in a village setting (hardly a town) of exceptional harmony, **2**, to which the bishops finally returned in 1242 after 154 years in the Roman artificiality of Bath. In the choir, transepts and nave, built gradually between 1180 and 1240 to a unified design, the cathedral was given the first Gothic building in England wholly of pointed arches (Canterbury choir and Chichester retrochoir still had some semicircular). Instead of the often illogical Purbeck shafting of Lincoln, Wells emphasized continuity of wall surfaces and continuity of mouldings. Aisle walls and arcade spandrels are flat and undivided, and the triforium is a continuous wall passage (not a gallery) with no capitals to its arches. The clustered pillars are so thick and closely set that they too read horizontally, and their capitals burst out in gorgeous blossoms of stiffleaf carving, the characteristic ornament of the English thirteenth century. Humorous grotesques such as the Apple Stealers are introduced into the flowing branches; but they are merely grotesque. Only the west front, with its harsh scaffolding of Purbeck marble shafts and its multitude of statues, disturbs the even harmony of Wells's naturalism; it is significant that Bishop Jocelyn who built it was a friend of Elias de Derham, the fanatical Purbeck shafter of Salisbury. In the superb north porch by contrast, **8**, mouldings intersect harmoniously against solid horizontal walling.

The thrill of Wells is its unity of connection not only of moulding to moulding and leaf to leaf but of building to building. The chapter house is placed at first floor level in a curious position on the opposite side from the cloisters. The staircase to it, **7**, of *c.* 1260, has wonderfully rippling steps which bifurcate romantically; one arm passes on, over the fifteenth century Chain Bridge, to the Vicars' Hall and Vicars' Close where the junior clergy lived; the other arm loops off into the chapter house itself which was not finished until *c.* 1310. By then another West Country cathedral, Exeter, had developed flowing Gothic to maturity by means of the 'palm branches' of tierceron ribs first introduced at Lincoln. Wells chapter house, **6**, has no fewer than thirty-two of these ribs outpouring from its central column.

The eastern transepts, retrochoir and Lady Chapel of the 'lower east end' type seem in outline as logical as Salisbury, except for the chapel's polygonal end. But spatially they are astonishingly varied and are a climax in Europe, not just in England, of the development of diagonal movement in place of the straight parallels of the basilica. The choir aisles have tierceron stars, the transepts elaborate lierne stars for their vaults, but these are still in square box-bays. Between them, however, six columns freely stand in the central space; they make the Lady Chapel an elongated octagon and they divide the lower retrochoir at right angles into an elongated hexagon and an irregular rectangle with left-over triangles at the sides. The result is indescribable; if it is the thrill of structure to be seen, it is the thrill of space to be unseen, like the wind — and only by analysing the vault can one see which way the wind is blowing. As Pevsner says, 'It is like penetrating a piece of complicated polyphonic music'. Polychromatically it is enhanced by the superb, if fragmentary, kaleidoscope of glass in the Lady Chapel. This is almost the only place where Wells has clustered Purbeck shafts; their small capitals are just sufficient for discipline, but not enough to break the flow.

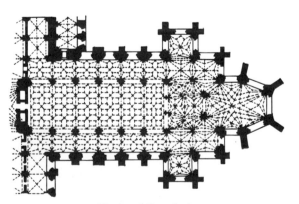

Vaults of East End

The choir itself was remodelled in *c.* 1330–45, and shows, **3**, in forms curious rather than attractive, the transition from the complete indeterminacy of Bristol (the lierne net vault) to the wiry perpendicular of Gloucester (the triforium panelling). The splendid central tower of 1315–22 which also prefigures Perpendicular (and had its windows made more so in *c.* 1440) had almost immediately to be propped up; and an engineering genius, perhaps brought from Bristol, produced the sensational solution of the inverted strainer arches, **4**. Continuously moulded with giant holes in the spandrels, they are a final proof that medieval architecture was unsentimental in its attitude to flowing nature.

The village precinct at Wells, **2**, is the beau ideal of the Saxon cathedral foundation. In the foreground are the Deanery, Chancellor's House and Archdeacon's House, with large gardens; next to them is the Vicars' Close with the so-called Chain Bridge linking it directly to the cathedral (see **7**, below); on the other side beyond the Bishop's Palace, the countryside runs directly up to the cathedral. Natural flowing forms are the essence of Wells's interior too; only in the choir, **3**, did the masons resort to surface patterning, which foreshadows the Perpendicular style. A stunning group of inverted strainer arches with giant bull's eye spandrels props up the central tower, **4**. Continuous mouldings without capitals had appeared in the triforium of the choir, transepts and nave of Wells from as early as 1180. The interlacing mouldings of the wall arcade in the north porch, **8**, shows a development of this search for flowing forms which reached its climax in the astonishing staircase, **7**, from the north transept to the Chain Bridge; half of it twists away independently into the superb chapter house, **6**, with its thirty-two branch 'palm tree' pier. Alabaster is a softly flowing material, typical of the later Middle Ages; the Dean Husee monument's panel of the Trinity, **5**, shows this flourishing export industry from Nottingham at its best.

2

3

4

5

6

7

8

The choir of Gloucester, **1**, begun in 1337, states the ultimate conclusion of English Gothic: the single room – not the clear-cut cube or double cube of the Renaissance such as Inigo Jones's at Wilton, but the boundless mystery of a Catholic heaven, in which the unity of structure is suffused from all sides with the indefinable light of stained glass. This is the mystical clarity which inspired the meditations of Juliana of Norwich and St John of the Cross; it only appears bare and plain now that the panoply of craftsmanship – glass, screens, paintings, statues – has largely gone.

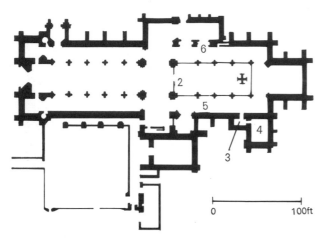

Bristol

The turning point architecturally was the choir at nearby Bristol, **2**, under way *c.* 1298–1330. The 'reticulated' net tracery of Wells was here developed into the elaborate and fantastical 'curvilinear' manner, with intersecting ogee arches and mouchettes (twisting dagger shapes) in the aisle windows. What matters at Bristol, however, is not the tracery patterns, but the three-dimensional spaces. For this is Europe's first Late Gothic 'hall church', with nave and aisles of equal height and continuous space – a type which in the fifteenth century became the progressive norm in Germany and Central Europe and, through German master-masons, in Spain.

The most obvious influence on Bristol's choir is the 'lower east end' type of retrochoir at Wells and Salisbury (and earlier still, at Winchester). The West of England parish churches, particularly in Devon and Cornwall, were meanwhile developing their characteristic single-storey, three-gabled form with continuous barrel roofs of wood. More important, and too easily forgotten because so few of their English churches survive, was the influence of the friars; they required big plain auditoria, and in Italy had arrived at a completely standardized single-storey layout of aisleless nave and tripartite chancel. The Bristol master-mason must also have seen (or seen drawings of) St Urbain at Troyes, the last great church of French High Gothic (*c.* 1261–77), where capitals were largely omitted from the arcades (as in the Wells nave triforium even earlier) and slim and wiry mouldings were made continuous throughout.

Bristol's choir and Lady Chapel are a single space, only 50 feet to the apex, and, apart from tiny capitals to the intentionally 'weightless' vaulting shafts, the wave mouldings of the arches are carried up and over in a single movement. The slender vaulting ribs rise not to the conventional ridge rib but (another touch of the weightless and ethereal) to a series of cusped kite shapes formed with ornamental lierne

ribs. The first lierne vaults, in Wells retrochoir and in the undercroft of St Stephen's, Westminster, were completed in *c.* 1319; their star shapes were used to throw separate bays into a single net. Because in a hall church it was not possible to carry the weight of the vault over the top of the aisles on flying buttresses, the Bristol master produced the brilliant solution of carrying it through the aisles on flying bridges, **5**, with thickly moulded mouchettes in the spandrels, reminiscent of the strainer arches at Wells. He then roofed the aisles in a series of transverse tunnel vaults and – the ultimate excitement – removed the cells of the vaulting immediately on top of each bridge; this leaves the ribs dancing on a tight-rope, with the single space of the east end flowing through on all sides.

Whereas Bristol achieved its spatial unity by acrobatically including the aisles in the overall impression of a single room, Gloucester firmly shut them out – unity by exclusion. Financed by pilgrimages to the tomb of Edward II, **9**, the entire east end was remodelled, **7** – but, typical of English pragmatism, not rebuilt. The inner faces of the Norman arcade and gallery were shaved off and hidden behind a continuous screen, **11**, of wiry uprights and horizontals (mullions and transoms) – the Perpendicular style in fact. Who invented it is not certain; it was used in the rebuilding of the Gloucester south transept (*c.* 1331–7), in the upper part of St Stephen's, Westminster (begun *c.* 1331) and in St Paul's Chapter House, begun in 1332 and designed by William of Ramsey. He became King's Chief Mason in 1336 and it is possible he was connected with Gloucester, as Edward III would have been closely interested in the shrine of his father.

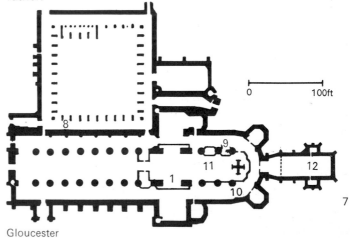

Gloucester

Behind the Gloucester grid the Norman aisles and triforium continue almost intact, **10** (as does almost the whole of the splendid nave). Continuously moulded vaulting shafts rise from the ground to support the starry firmament of lierne vaulting, **1**, which covers the whole room without differentiation of bay from bay. The east wall is also a single element: a colossal (72 feet by 38 feet) stained glass memorial to those who fell at Crécy (1346). The shadows lurking behind it are the Norman corner chapels, the Lady Chapel added in Perpendicular's maturity (*c.* 1457–83), **12**, and the triforium which boldly carries round as a bridge at the back of the chapel. The ultimate single rooms of Perpendicular Gothic were the royal chapels for King's College, Cambridge, and Henry VII's tomb at Westminster; for them another invention at Gloucester was crucial: the use in the cloisters (from *c.* 1370) of fan vaulting, **8**.

1

3

2

The sensational lightness and transparency of the Bristol choir, **2**, is played up by the heavily static Victorian reredos by Pearson. Whereas at Wells, in the retrochoir, the spatial complexity was still clarified by a conventional use of the elements of Gothic arches, the Bristol master-mason eliminated the capital, minimized the plinth and brought the single storey continuity of retrochoirs into the main vessel of a church. The mouldings are extremely delicate ; the only vestige of a capital is on the very thin vaulting shafts, so thin that they could never carry the vault. The vault compounds this insecurity by breaking off the ribs just

4

where they would normally be tied firmly together at the ridge; instead, a series of cupped kite shapes are formed with the small non-structural ribs called liernes. The lierne vault had been invented ten years earlier at either Wells or St Stephen's, Westminster. Since the aisles had been brought up to the full height of the choir, there was no possibility of carrying the weight of the chancel vault over the top of them by means of flying buttresses; so the Bristol master-mason adopted the outré solution of 'flying bridges', 5. On each bridge rest the sides of two little transverse barrel vaults; and here the surprise is that the two vaulting

5

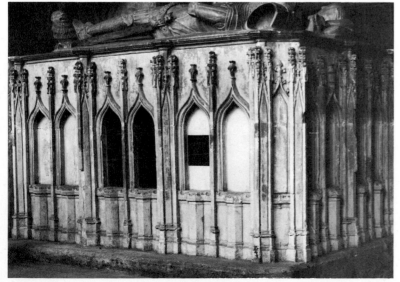

6

cells immediately on top of each bridge were left out, so as to leave each vault pirouetting on a point, with vistas flowing through. In the antechapel to the Berkeley Chapel, south of the choir, all the vaulting cells are left out of a simple cross ribbed vault, 3 – a kind of structural expression more familiar to us in reinforced concrete. The tomb of Thomas Lord Berkeley, 4, has its tomb chest decorated in a surprising combination of heraldry and foliage enclosed by three-quarter circles joined together. The slightly later monument to Maurice Lord Berkeley, died 1368, rejects such aggressively over-scaled ornament and adopts instead slender ogee arches, 6, that look more like Strawberry Hill Gothick of the eighteenth century than the genuine article. The nave of Bristol, incidentally, was barely started in the Middle Ages; what we see now is a conscientious attempt at the style of the choir by G. E. Street, begun in 1868.

Hagiology of ever more fantastic kinds was a major part of popular religion in the fourteenth and fifteenth centuries; but there can have been few more unlikely saints than King Edward II. He was a weak-minded man, civilized enough to prefer gardening to jousting. After his murder in Berkeley Castle his body was refused by Bristol's monks because of their Berkeley benefactions, but soon after it arrived in Gloucester there were reports of miracle-working at the tomb – which itself soon became one of the most beautiful of medieval canopied shrines, **9**. Out of the proceeds of pilgrimage, Gloucester (then an abbey) rebuilt its cloisters, **8**, with the attractive invention of fan-vaulting, and remodelled its entire east end. Externally, **7**, this has all the clarity of Perpendicular: south transept and choir added, central tower rebuilt and Lady Chapel added, in that chronological order. The survival of the Norman turrets flanking the transept window should make the visitor wary that not all is as clear as it seems. In fact almost the whole structure of the twelfth-century choir survives, including the aisles, the apsidal chapels and the uniquely usable triforium, **10**. The master-mason, whoever he was (William of Ramsey has been suggested on the strength

7

8

9

of his proto-Perpendicular chapter house at Old St Paul's), took the structure as he found it, shaving off and remoulding its internal face. Between continuously moulded vaulting-shafts he applied a consistent network of Perpendicular panelling, **11**, consciously scaleless, to break up the previous three-storey elevation. The details are hard and brittle but the total space is magnificent, because the designer concentrated his resources on providing an apparently aiseless room with a glittering net of lierne vaulting and a totally glazed east wall. The triforium is carried round behind the east window in the form of a bridge across the west end of the Lady Chapel, **12**. The chapel follows the same general lines as the choir, emphasizing the connection between Gloucester and the single room royal chapels of the late fifteenth century (King's, Eton, and Henry VII's at Westminster).

10

11

12

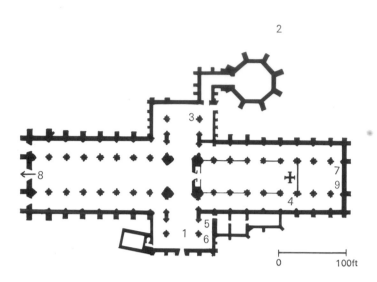

The primary aim of stained glass is not to tell a story, but to change the colour of the light entering a building, so creating an atmosphere of divine presence. It is only in the overall context of this 'heavenly' light that we can appreciate the detailed Poor Man's Bible of saints and martyrs. York Minster has ancient glass in almost every window, 117 in all; and it provides a unique opportunity to chart all the main changes in artistic and religious taste from 1160 to 1550.

Architecturally there are only two parts of York which live up to their acreage: the transepts, **1**, and the Chapter House, **2**. Archbishop de Grey's south transept of *c.* 1220–41 is the summit of that Northern Gothic which began at Tynemouth and Hexham; the ruined choirs of Whitby and Rievaulx have the same spirited shafting and excessively emphasized galleries. The bay next to the crossing is curiously asymmetrical; the reason is that the narrow Norman crossing (of which there are still fragments high up in the gallery) was not replaced until William of Colchester's dignified central tower was built in 1407–23. Only then was the vista opened fully to the north transept (*c.* 1245–60), culminating in the wonderful window known as the Five Sisters, with its double mullioned lancets 53 feet high, **3**. Next to it is the entrance to the chapter house (*c.* 1286–1307), a majestic octagonal room with an umbrella vault of wood balanced precariously without the usual central pillar. The rippling stone canopies of the canons's stalls, with their sculptured pendants, are a Northern response to the spatial complexity of Bristol and Wells.

Otherwise it is the glass that matters. The earliest panel of all survives in the second window from the west in the north aisle: a Byzantinizing figure of a king from a Jesse window of *c.* 1160. It comes from the cathedral of Bishop Roger de Pont l'Evêque, of which some stubby Durham-like columns survive in the crypt; close to them is a savagely admonitory sculpture of the Jaws of Hell known as the Doom Stone.

The Five Sisters window is entirely abstract. It is the finest surviving example in England of *grisaille* glass – patterning in grey (as the name suggests) with touches of green and yellow, spots of red, and a leaf pattern in brown, different in each panel. Shortly afterwards (*c.* 1270) some windows

were put into the Norman nave, which were then re-used when rebuilding started in 1291. The five panels of the Redemption, **5** and **6**, moved again to the south transept, are possibly the finest glass in the cathedral, the equivalent of Lincoln's Angel Choir in sculpture: strong abstract panels in deep colours (reds, greens, yellows), enclosing figures either statuesque or flowing.

The majority of glass in the nave, however, dates from its completion in *c.* 1310–45. The west window's flowing tracery of 1338, with its curious palm-branched heart shape, has rich tiers of architectural canopies and of red and yellow saints, **8**. The west window of the south aisle, presented by Thomas de Beneston in 1338, has a noble Crucifixion of that extremely elongated and emaciated kind which shows the English passion for linear design. In all these windows and above all in the superb Jesse Tree of *c.* 1310 in the south aisle the lines of the leading are used as strongly in the patterning as the actual coloured quarries. At the apex of the Jesse sits a grave and noble Madonna, seated within a green and red frame, and connected to the other figures by the vine branches which epitomize the flowing line of the fourteenth century. Light is let into the church through interstices of whitish grisaille, between the figure panels. The edges of the windows are decorated with intricate borders of foliage and animals.

Hagiology was meanwhile developing as an elaborate superstructure of religious observance. The nave, for example, contains scenes of the life of St Nicholas of Myra and St John when Bishop of Ephesus. In the famous window depicting the craft of bellfounding, the completed bell is presented to the local patron, St William of York, whose body was transferred to an elaborate shrine behind the High Altar in 1284; he was an inferior Becket – a persecuted twelfth-century archbishop. The whole east end of the cathedral was rebuilt in *c.* 1361–1425 with the same majestic spaces and thin detailing as in the nave (the main vaults are of timber). The stained glass gradually became less strong in pattern and in colour, and concentrated more on story telling; the windows were merely luminous paintings hung on the walls.

The enormous east window, however, achieves a final synthesis, combining the new delicacy of line and of tonal shading with all the old virtues. It was made by an outsider, John Thornton of Coventry, in 1405–8. As with the Five Sisters, double mullions are used. **4**, giving more depth to the window's luminosity. In the tracery, below myriad figures of angels, patriarchs, prophets, and saints, there are three bands of Old Testament scenes, in which the Days of Creation, **9**, are depicted with particularly vigorous patterning. The main part of the windows shows the myth of the Apocalypse. In the scene of St John the Divine sailing to Patmos, **7**, there is a contrast characteristic of English Gothic in the semi-abstract vigour of the ship and the weak fluffiness of the human figure.

It is interesting to compare these panels with the wholly painterly approach of the early sixteenth century Renaissance, in the panels depicting the legend of Gilbert Becket (probably made locally by Flemish immigrants), **10**, and in the Crucifixion from St Jean at Rouen presented to the cathedral by its late Dean, Eric Milner-White. It was he who after the last war took the opportunity to restore the evacuated windows before putting them back in again; in many cases his scholarship and devotion, interpreted by the Minster's own three glaziers, turned a ruinous maze into an almost perfect work of art.

On the north side of the Minster, **2**, the stern simplicity of the Five Sisters and the Chapter House is matched by the central tower. Inside, the Five Sisters' intricate mosaic of grisaille glass is given extra depth, **3**, by the use of double mullions; this is also used for the two lower tiers of John Thornton's great east window, **4**. High Gothic glass of *c*. 1270 is shown superbly in the panels of the Annunciation, **5**, and the Resurrection, **6**, from a series of five brought down recently from the nave clerestory to five lancets in the east wall of the south transept. The delicacy of the female figures contrasts with the chunky masculinity of the Risen Christ. The more easily flowing, more painterly style of the west window (*c*. 1330) is beautifully illustrated in the evangelist St John, **8**. In Thornton's east

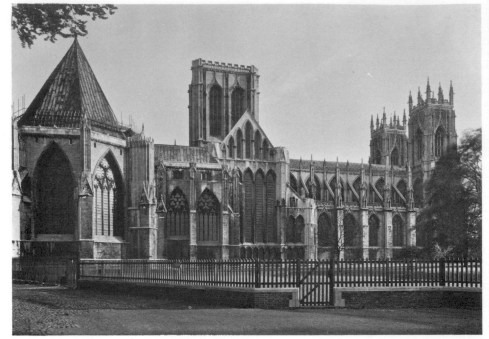

2

3

4

5

6

7

8

9

10

window (1405–8), the strength of the leading and the richness of the colours are magnificently sustained: St John sailing to Patmos, 7, is the second of eighty-one scenes from the Apocalypse in the main part of the window. The climax, however, is the group of twenty-seven Old Testament scenes in the tracery, beginning with almost abstract scenes of the Creation, such as the Third Day, 9, with its stylized trees and herbs. The majority of the windows at the east end are in a much slacker fifteenth-century style, pale in colour. Of the final phase, contemporary with Flemish windows at King's College, Cambridge, York has an excellent example, 10, in a series of windows of c. 1535, partly in the Minster and partly in the adjoining church of St Michael-le-Belfrey, depicting the legend of Gilbert Becket (father of Thomas).

St Paul's is not one of the ideal buildings of the Renaissance: it is the grandiose result of a typically English, and Anglican, series of compromises between Catholic mystery and Protestant auditorium. When the organ still stood on a central screen, 1, the interior was remarkably similar in layout to Ely Cathedral, where Sir Christopher Wren's uncle was Bishop.

Old St Paul's had been the largest of all medieval English cathedrals: 596 feet long with a spire 489 feet high, which was struck by lightning in 1561. It had a long Norman nave, used profanely for public business as Paul's Walk, and an immense twelve bay chancel based on Lincoln and Westminster. Its most important feature was the Chapter House of 1332, in the centre of a small southern cloister; it was designed by William of Ramsey as one of the earliest Perpendicular buildings.

Under Bishop Laud, the Royalist High Churchman, Inigo Jones began belated repairs in 1634, 2, removing shops and houses that abutted, scraping off the pinnacles and tracery of the nave in favour of plain classical mouldings, and adding the magnificent Corinthian portico at the west end (the gift of Charles I). After acting as cavalry barracks in the Civil War, St Paul's was again in decay; a Royal Commission appointed in 1663 asked for a survey from Dr Christopher Wren, the young astronomer who had just completed the Sheldonian Theatre at Oxford. He recommended in 1666 that the nave's interior should be classicised as well and that a domed 'rotundo' should replace the central tower. Within a few months the Great Fire gutted it all; but, because of false hopes of restoration, it was not until 1668 that Wren was commissioned to prepare plans for an entirely new building.

Wren made four designs in all. His first one was Protestant and curious: a big oblong auditorium, entered through a domed narthex, with galleries extending outside it over cloisters, which would provide the same secular facilities as Paul's Walk. His second design, 3, the Great Model (which still exists, 18 feet long) was of a much better scale and reflected expertly the up-to-date classicism of the Catholic churches (at the Sorbonne and Val-de-Grace) that Wren would have seen on his Paris visit in 1665. A domed narthex with Corinthian portico led into a vast domed space on eight arches; the four Greek cross arms were connected by concave quadrant curves. The design 'pleased persons of distinction, skilled in antiquity and architecture', but the clergy would not have it: because it was impossible to build slowly in phases as money came in, and because the Restoration Establishment needed reassurance about its apostolic succession from the medieval Ecclesia Anglicana — paradoxical conservatism for a 'reformed' Church in view of the excesses of originality Borromini could unleash on 'unreformed' Rome.

Wren then 'turned his thoughts to a cathedral form, as they called it, but so rectified as to reconcile as near as possible the Gothick to a better Manner of Architecture'. The result was the weird Warrant Design: a nave and choir with transepts and lower aisles in the medieval way, and a central 'rotundo' surmounted by an elongated dome with a pagoda-type spire on top. The king approved it as 'very artificial, proper and useful', but fortunately gave Wren an 'escape clause' to make 'variations rather ornamental than essential, as from time to time he shall see proper'.

Wren's Warrant design, 1675

The final building (1675–1710) follows Ely even closer than the Warrant design: as well as the Latin Cross plan with a big central space, there are also western transept chapels. Externally there are convincing improvements. The elevation was made two-storeyed, the upper level of niches in aedicules (deriving from Jones's strict Palladianism) being an almost complete sham, hiding the neo-medieval expedient of flying buttresses. The western portico lost its giant order, 5, as Portland stone could not be quarried in sufficient lengths, and a rather weak two-tier system took its place; the western towers, however, were at a later stage (c. 1705) transformed into brilliantly agitated Baroque cupolas, possibly to the design of Wren's long-time assistant, Nicholas Hawksmoor. The dome by contrast ended serenely; only the breaking of its continuous colonnade by occasional buttresses is Baroque — particularly as the niched ends of these buttresses are in a different coloured stone (golden Ketton). The dome itself is of three layers, 4: a brick inner skin with Thornhill's murals, a timber and lead outer skin, and between them a brick cone supporting the Baroque lantern.

Internally the compromise is less happy. The nave and aisles are domed and clerestoried uniformly in each sonorous bay; but the system is lost in the supports to the dome, where the divergence in size of arches could only be resolved across the aisles by the awkward arrangement of a semicircular arch above a segmental arch. The latest brand of High Churchmanship, the Oxford Movement, persuaded the Chapter in 1872 to remove the organ screen (the organ was then divided above the choir stalls, 7), so as to provide a continuous vista to the altar, where a Baroque baldacchino has recently replaced the Bodley and Garner's stodgy Italianate reredos of 1880. Meanwhile the transepts had become littered with frigid marbles to Peninsular war heroes. Fortunately the crypt has since been used as a pantheonic catacomb; it includes busts by Rodin and Epstein, the Duke of Wellington's funeral carriage of 1852 designed by Gottfried Semper, and the gorgeous black marble Renaissance sarcophagus made by Benedetto da Rovezzano in 1524–9 for Cardinal Wolsey but now housing the body of Horatio Lord Nelson — the strangest compromise of all.

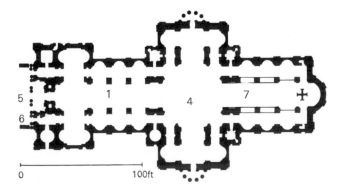

5
6
1
4
7

0   100ft

By the seventeenth century Old St Paul's, the largest medieval English cathedral, was in a state of collapse. Inigo Jones scraped most of the tracery and pinnacles off the exterior, **2**, and added a pure Corinthian portico to the west front for Bishop Laud (1634–42). Wren prepared schemes for further propping it up, both before and after the Great Fire gutted it.

When commissioned for a new building, he first proposed a simple oblong auditorium with galleries, and then in the Second Model Design a centrally planned Renaissance church, **3**, with an almost separate domed narthex. Turned down both times by the conservative clergy, he produced the Warrant Design (see page 34) which was based on a medievalizing

2

3

4

5

6

plan with a crazy pagoda-like steeple; he got permission to build it but had no intention of doing so. An 'escape clause' allowed him to produce his final compromise: a medieval plan similar to Ely, which is nevertheless convincingly classical from certain viewpoints. The splendid dome, 4, is effective externally and internally by adopting an aesthetic sleight of hand in both cases; the actual structure is a brick cone which supports the lantern. The west front, 5, is frankly romantic in its grouping: a traditional twin-towered west front set at an angle to Ludgate Hill, with no broad vistas intended and with dramatic use of sculpture by Francis Bird and other masons on the skyline, 6. The quality of the masonry throughout St Paul's is superb. The recent cleaning has revealed the extent to which Wren was able to 'sell' Baroque religious sculpture to a supposedly Protestant nation. Grinling Gibbons's choir stalls, 7, with Jean Tijou's wrought iron gates, are similarly designed for display and fit in well with the conspicuously High Church mosaics added by the Victorians in the spandrels and vaults.

7

Until last summer's spoliation at Birmingham, the two Midland cathedrals of St Chad were the most perfect Victorian cathedral interiors by two great masters, Augustus Welby Pugin and Sir George Gilbert Scott. Each tackled in a characteristically different way the vexed question of screens — a central problem for a century which initiated mass education and so encouraged a growing demand for popular participation in church services.

Even the 'single-space' medieval cathedrals such as Gloucester and Bristol had always been two spaces: the nave for the people and the choir for the Chapter. Between them stood a massive stone screen, or pulpitum, which shut off the people from all except a distant chanting and murmuring. There were, however, a number of nave altars — until the Anglican reformers made matters worse by abolishing them and then allowing a select group of churchgoers to sit up with the canons. With the Victorian religious revival there was bound to be a reaction: more cathedral screens were thrown out in c. 1830–50 than by Cromwell's Puritans. The removal of screens was often done for the purely picturesque reason of 'opening up vistas' — yet it almost always ruined the true character of a Gothic cathedral, which is additive and compartmental.

'Ambonoclast' (screen destroyer) was the furious label Pugin stuck on his opponents. Though half French by birth, he was a convert of converts, moved by white hot zeal for the Faith. His fellow-converts sadly disappointed him; they turned out to have Italophile, operatic and ultramontane tastes which were even more anti-screen than the Anglicans. Yet for Pugin the rood screen was the essence of Gothic mystery. His most sympathetic patrons were the Old Catholic families. The Earl of Shrewsbury had introduced him to Birmingham's Oscott seminary, where he became Professor of Ecclesiastical Antiquities and delivered his series of slashing lectures entitled *An Apology for the Revival of Pointed or Christian Architecture.*

St Chad's, built in 1839–41 as a cheap pro-cathedral, raises its clean brick masses and slender North German spires on a hillside, 4, where once they dominated the cottages of the jewellers' quarter — now swept away for the Inner Ring Road, together with Pugin's strikingly original brick Bishop's House. Germany also gave Pugin the late medieval (post-Bristol) idea of a 'hall church' with exquisitely tall pillars, 3, as ascetic in structure as a friars' church. The gilded and painted wooden rood screen was the centrepiece, 3, until it was broken down last summer to make St Chad's 'conform' (though its longitudinal spaces never can) to recent Vatican

directives on Liturgy. On it were eight ancient statues, part of a rich haul of genuine medieval art presented by Lord Shrewsbury and interwoven by Pugin with his own convincing revivalism. The superb pulpit, 6, with statues of the Latin Doctors, is from St Gertrude, Louvain; the archbishop's throne and his choir stall from St Maria in Cosmedin, Cologne; and the stalls also from Cologne. In the apse, 1, the glass is by William Warrington, Pugin's first collaborator before he met John Hardman, the Birmingham metalworker, who became the leading layman at St Chad's.

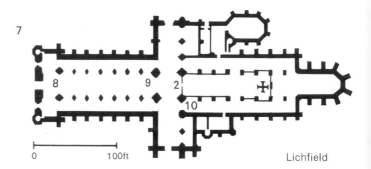

Lichfield

Scott was by contrast a born compromiser; and in the synthetic art of architecture that can sometimes lead to a masterpiece. As at Hereford, where his screen was removed last spring, Scott at Lichfield employed cast iron, 2, slim and strong and filigree, to define the traditional separation of a screen while at the same time allowing the congregation a panoramic view through it. Francis Skidmore of Coventry made it, augmenting it with wrought iron, polished brass and semi-precious stones. Next to it is the wonderful pulpit, 9, an openwork cage with two separate flights of stairs, almost Baroque in layout. Scott also designed monuments to Bishop Lonsdale (effigy by G. F. Watts) and Dean Howard (effigy by H. H. Armstead), a new reredos with many encrusted niches and a new set of choir stalls.

As a whole Lichfield is the most satisfying Victorian cathedral we have. The medieval building is still there in outline: thirteenth-century choir, transepts, chapter house and nave; west front of 1280–1327 and Lady Chapel of c. 1320–45; and the three slim spires of the late fourteenth century, 7. But it was all shot up in the Civil War and then botched in its repairs under Bishop Hacket (1661–9) and by James Wyatt (1788–95). Scott restored it conscientiously and learnedly from end to end. Of the nave he said 'I always hold this work to be almost absolute perfection in design and details' — and it is as perfection restored that he has left it to us, 8. The high Lady Chapel, in losing its Wyatt stucco, has been given a rocky Victorian texture in stone which recalls Scott's own Exeter College Chapel at Oxford.

As a bonus, other architects were employed: Sidney Smirke (architect of the British Museum reading room) restored the south aisle; William Slater did the font, left in 8; and George Edmund Street produced, at the peak of his career, the adventurous French Gothic tomb to a youth killed at Lucknow, 10. The side aisles share a feature with Birmingham: just as John Hardman's firm put up many small brass inscriptions at Birmingham to the Catholic faithful, so at Lichfield the wall arcading in the aisles, after an improbable peppering of Grecian white marble, came to be peppered still more with an extraordinary array of little brass plates in elaborate Gothic script, which someone some day is sure to wish to rub.

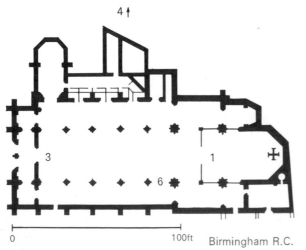

Birmingham R.C.

1

2

3

4

A contrast in settings: Pugin's Baltic spires of St Chad's and his Bishop's House (since demolished), seen from Snow Hill station platform, **4**, and the peaceful Close at Lichfield, **7**, overlooked by the three spires and Scott's hardboiled rebuilding of the west front. At a cost of barely £20,000, Pugin achieved in the soaring arcades of St Chad's, **3**, the passionate simplicity of a friars' church; his gilded screen has recently been removed as part of a com-

5

6

7

8

promise re-ordering; Pugin's own uncompromising approach to the minutiæ of a medieval liturgy is well illustrated, **5**, in his frontispiece to *A Missal for the Laity*, 1843. Scott by contrast was at his best when compromising; his openwork iron screens made by Skidmore, **8**, were an effective solution to the problem of reconciling inherited medieval plans such as Lichfield with the growing demand for participation in the services (note font on left by William Slater, 1862). Pugin's pulpit, **6**, is the real thing, made in the fifteenth century for St Gertrude, Louvain; whereas Scott's pulpit, **9**, is a brilliant metal cage created by himself and Francis Skidmore. A striking High Victorian tomb, designed by George Edmund Street, **10**, for a young man killed at Lucknow, stands close to Scott's splendid screen; it shows the fearless absorption by High Victorian architects of Continental influences.

9

10

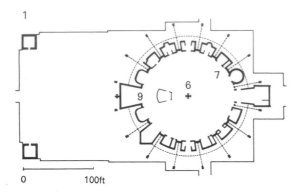

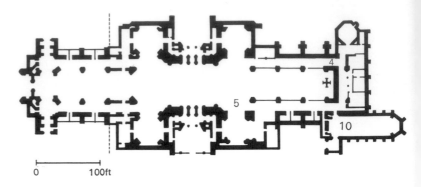

Liverpool, R.C.

Liverpool, Anglican

Sir Frederick Gibberd's skeletal tent, **1**, perched on the massive platform of Lutyens's crypt, has a challenging relationship with Sir Giles Gilbert Scott's Catalan Gothic splendour further along the ridge, **2**. One is a monument to popular Irish Catholicism, the other to the Protestant ascendancy of shipowners; one leaps athletically on naked concrete clad only in thin white mosaic, the other stands massively on millions of bricks robed in thousands of tons of pink sandstone. Scott won the Anglican competition in 1902, Gibberd the Catholic in 1960; yet it is Gibberd's design that is already complete while Scott's still lacks its nave and west front. Both were intended essentially as single spaces for communal worship and both approached this task in an essentially monumental way in the Gothic tradition.

The central space of the Anglican Cathedral is quite as big as that of the Roman Catholic. Bishop Chavasse laid it down in the competition conditions that gatherings of up to three thousand people should be provided for and, as Chavasse was an Evangelical, preached at. Scott at first produced a strangely additive arrangement of cells in the Yorkshire Gothic of his master, Temple Moore; but when the aged G. F. Bodley was appointed to superintend the twenty-two-year-old Scott, the Lady Chapel retreated into beautifully lacy screen work, **10**. Bodley died in 1907; and Scott then proceeded to do a complete redesigning in which the twin towers on a single transept, **3**, became a single tower over an enormous central space between two transepts, **2**. Of the two ceremonial porches, that in **2** is wholly redundant.

The thrill of Scott's cathedral is purely spatial: the vast height of the central space (175 feet to the peak of the vault) with its converging arches, **5**, all perfectly controlled in scale. The use of the same sandstone blocks throughout in big areas of blank walling, **4**, gives the eye a vocabulary of scale, which can be picked out and understood at any height. But what happens in this space? Row upon row of chairs in fact march axially away to the High Altar which is at the far end of the distant chancel. As Chavasse intended, the pulpit is in the centre; it is surely only a matter of time before the altar is moved there too. Recently a movable nave altar has been inserted, to the design of G. G. Pace; and the opportunity could be taken to expel the plethora of trite furnishings — sentimental stained glass, neon-Gothic light fittings, knobbly literature desks.

Whereas Scott's exterior is purely a pictorial massif, Gibberd has intelligently used the site to restate the external message of a Catholic shrine: geometrical temple on panoramic platform on sacred hilltop. Already on the site was the nearly completed crypt of Sir Edwin Lutyens's gigantic Byzantine cathedral designed in 1930. (Edward – son of – Pugin's cathedral of 1855 at Everton had never progressed beyond the Lady Chapel; Adrian – brother of – Gilbert Scott's diluted Lutyens design of 1953 was rightly discarded). Gibberd has used it, **1**, as the platform of an 'open air basilica' with its altar backed up against the picture frame end of the Blessed Sacrament Chapel. The tent itself, with its lantern rising out of the Sanctuary, is a much more logical expression of its interior than Scott's tower (which is separated from the space below it by a vault). In his letter to competitors, Cardinal Heenan said: 'The high altar is not an ornament to embellish the cathedral building. The cathedral on the contrary is built to enshrine the altar of sacrifice'. The result is oddly similar to the Octagon at Ely (*cf.* St Paul's). It has been suggested that Gibberd consciously imitated Oscar Niemeyer's unfinished 'wigwam' cathedral at Brasilia; but in fact the prominent flying buttresses were an afterthought suggested by the structural engineer, James Lowe. Gibberd decided, following Heenan's words, to place the altar directly in the centre with the building revolving round, **7**, and that is a sufficient explanation of the shape. However, it is rather a naïve expression of the 'church-in-the-round': the priest who faces across the altar to the people rather than away from the people to the altar does not need a whole quadrant of a circle to move about in.

Where Gibberd's cathedral is uncertain is in its sense of scale. The superb lantern of glass by John Piper and Patrick Reyntiens, **6**, is not strongly tied to earth. The concrete frame is so thin that bright blue glass at the lower levels overshadows it; and the need to cover the chapel walls in acoustic plaster, rather than the stone courses shown in the original drawings, causes a lack of identity and definition. The clustering of chapels between the buttresses which is so effective externally is simply confusing internally, and their 'standard modern' furnishings — no less trite than Scott's — fail to assert any meaningful symbolism, **9**.

But what *is* meaningful today? Will these two proud crowns on the skyline, **8**, bring the pilgrims flocking? Perhaps they will be the last of their size and ambition to do so. Coventry has already shown that more can be done pastorally in the outhouses of a cathedral precinct — in small meetings and meals, which is what worship used to be — than in the grand-slam services for thousands. The informal Saxon monastery is still rebelling against designs from outsiders.

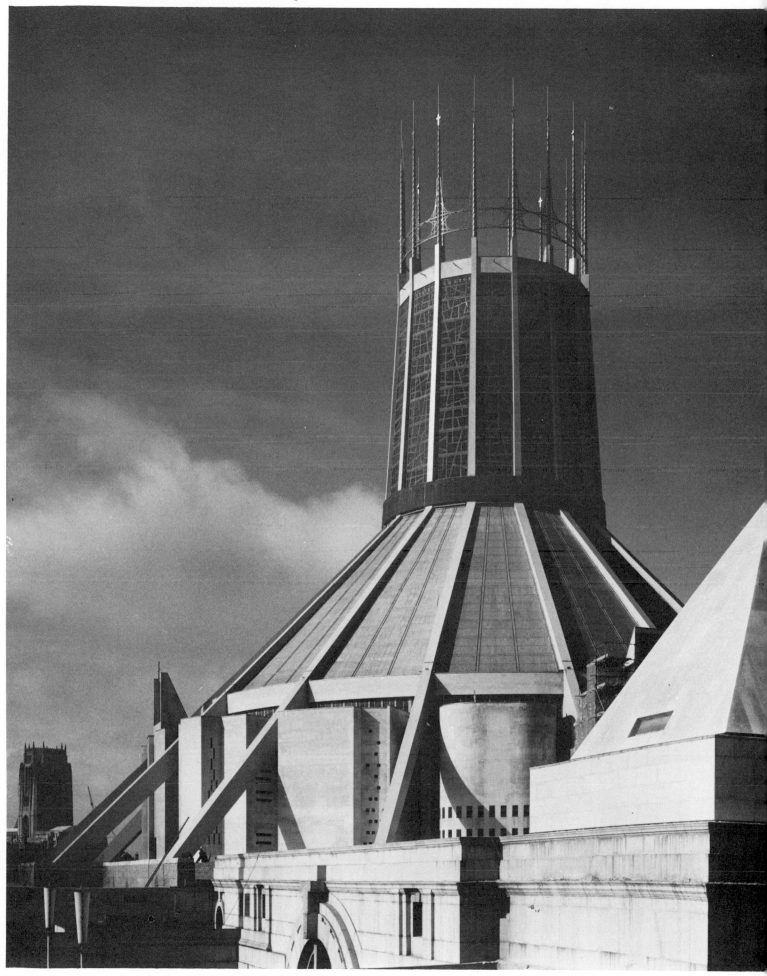

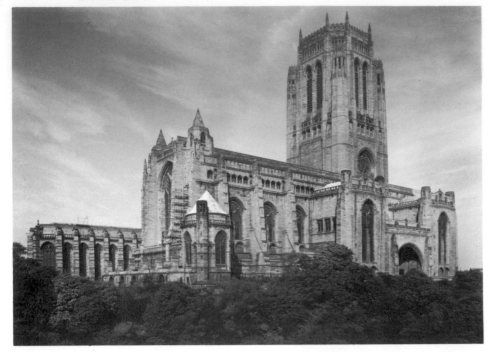

2

Rising out of the trees of a decayed Regency cemetery, **2**, the unfinished Anglican cathedral is a vast pink sandstone pile, with green copper roofs. The executed design of a single central tower flanked by double transepts was adopted in 1910, the year the Lady Chapel (projecting on left of **2**) was opened. Scott's competition-winning design of 1902, **3**, had a single transept with two towers on it. The heart of the new design is the central congregational space under the tower, **5**, daringly supported on the two side walls which are nevertheless pierced with large windows and entrance doors. The two transverse arches are 107 feet high. The first two bays of the nave and the bridge across (a spectacular view-

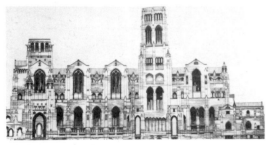

3

4

6

point) were opened in 1961. Scott never faltered in his consistent use of sandstone inside and out. Whereas his furnishings show that Gothic was played out as a language of detailed design, his bare wall surfaces, 4, are timeless in their instinctive handling of scale, dramatized by concealed lighting. Sir Frederick Gibberd by contrast has a single flexible space crowned by the all-pervading stained glass lantern of Piper and Reyntiens, 6, in itself a superb piece of abstract and atmospheric design. It is related to the central sanctuary, 7, by the baldacchino of aluminium tubing. The side-chapels, framed in bright blue glass, have indefinite surfaces of acoustic plaster. Liverpool must be unique in the world in having its

7

8

9

skyline dominated, **8**, by two such formidable modern cathedrals. Are they signs of piety or are they merely the dying gasp of the medieval monument (pre-ecumenically in allowing *two* such cathedrals)? It is interesting to compare the changes of taste in sixty years from the Lady Chapel, **10**, strongly influenced by Spanish Gothic and by G. F. Bodley, an assessor of the competition, who was initially appointed to assist the twenty-two-year-old Scott, to Gibberd's Chapel of the Blessed Sacrament, **9**, which has an abstract reredos and stained glass by Ceri Richards.

10